Midnight Musings

SNIGDHA DALMIYA NATHANY

BookLeaf Publishing

India | USA | UK

Presentation by *BookLeaf Publishing*

Web: www.bookleafpub.com

E-mail: info@bookleafpub.com

ISBN: 9789363316966

First edition 2024

Serendipity

When there's a bounce in my steps,
And my spirits soar high
When I breathe free,
And leap towards the sky
When the wind is in my hair,
And the breeze tickles my feet,
The cruel crusader of ennui,
Catches me unaware
It stretches out its clutches and pulls me down
It jerks me up and turns me around
It tackles me, mauls me, to roughly hover
And rob me off of all my fervor.

When the real world loses meaning
And utopia takes over
When imagination churns like wheels

And my eyes seek cover
I be the princess, the villain and the hero
The world's my stage
I am the poet, the tycoon, the guru
This is when, through the cracks in my soul
Toxic reality seeps in like pain
It divulges and creeps onto obscure crevices
It leaves me numb, it leaves me slain.

When someday I wake up with a 'feeling'
When I don't think about the day and nothing
seems compelling
When spongy decadence engulfs my mind
I feel a stark iciness, difficult to describe
As it eats away rationality
It oozes out pleasure
That's when reason stealthily comes my way
It stops short, emanating the heat of the day
It embraces me tight injecting its warmth
My pleasure drips away
As it burns in my mind's hearth.

Sometimes when my strength finds body
My will finds soul
My nerves find steel
Making me one whole
When I feel edgy and ready to take a risk
To climb a mountain, to jump off a cliff
I am weighed down by colossal fear

Like tumbling rocks in my heart,
Making my brain hard to steer
If I take a step forward
I move back by two
I am always on the verge, always dreaming
But still stagnant, cause they never come true.

When the world takes a new shape
When I see all good
When life seems like a blessing
And people better than they should
When optimism becomes my virtue
And peace my mental state
A negative thought casually enters, its eyes
shining with hate
It stares into my perfect spectacle
Drowning itself into my eyes
My mind clouds over, ringing with a violent din
And it can't get rid of it however hard it tries.

But once in my life, a day unfolds like no other
There's no boredom, life's not a drag
When I look back, fear is no bother
I find pleasure in the smallest things
I feel positive with no misgivings
Life flows smooth
Like slathering buttercream on my skin
I cut through the day
Like a melted marshmallow ring

I glide forward
Like an ice princess on skates
I bob along
Missing all dangerous baits
When I am in a car, the traffic melts away
As I go ahead, all obstructions give way
I fall on the ground, only to spring back higher
I stand dazzling at the world's grand foyer
When I want something, it's right before my
eyes
When someone wants me, I get a message from
the skies
Life flares like a crescendo, getting better with
every beat
It bursts with bouts of hue, achieving a colorful
feat
When things tone down, nothing is bitter
The grandeur is replaced by the bird's twitter
The simplicity of life shines like crystal
innocence
When nature hugs you, it dims out all opulence
Oh! If I could stand by a life so charmed
I could endure wars, strutting about unarmed.

When I think about losing this life, my insides
cringe
It has fit into a socket, I don't want it to unhinge
But when I think about it hard
My mind picks up a wise shard

That if I hadn't known the dismal life
The unpleasant times, the bitter strife
The blessed existence that I got to see
Would have held no value to me
Life is about contrast, difference and
dissimilarity
You have to know one side to comprehend the
other's clarity
Life is about cracks and bumps
About saddles and humps
About ups and downs, rise and fall
But a day of serendipity makes up for all.

The Turncoat that is Life

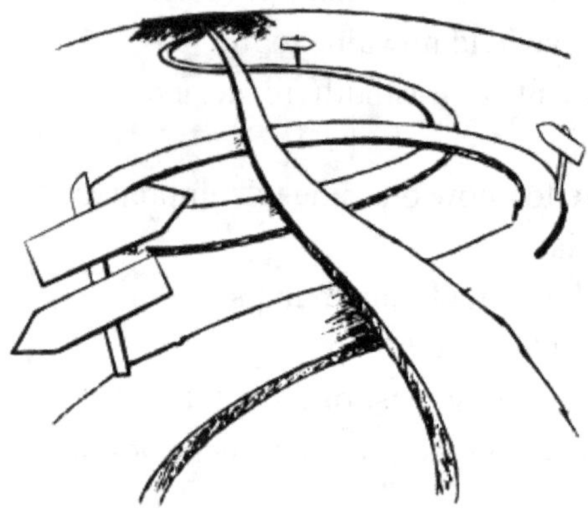

Sometimes when I look at the horizon expecting
a golden spill to stain the sky,
I find a dullness so somber that it fogs all hope
in my eye.
Sometimes when I turn back expecting to see a
familiar crowd,
I see only strangers against a bedlam; garish and
loud.
Sometimes when I eagerly wait for results which
could go either way,
Why is it that they always go astray?
But when sometimes I expect a catastrophe,
An abhorrent disaster, a mind-numbing tragedy,
I find a deviation so surreal,
Like a beautiful dream; distant and ephemeral.

Or when sometimes my mind believes,
That a person is nasty, with malice up his
sleeves,
He turns out to be an answer to a prayer,
So clean, so virtuous, so untaintedly fair.
Or when sometimes a mail arrives
And sad expectations cut through the air like
knives,
I am grabbed by a pleasantness so new,
When out comes a sweet-smelling Billet Doux.
Life is a poltergeist, a player of sorts,
It springs on you unexpectedly and playfully
snorts.
"Hope for the best!" is the wisdom people tend
to offer,
But with a jostle or two with life, I beg to differ.

Mindnumb

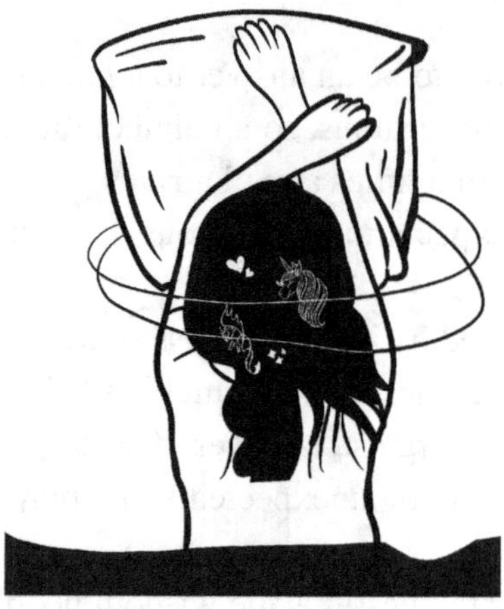

I stand awash with guilt,
A restless gnawing in the back of my mind,
Squinting my vision to avoid rationality,
In a smothered buzz,
In cerebral slumber.
I am alert,
Cognizant of all,

Yet brandishing everything of import,
In frivolous fiesta,
In paltry haze.

I am sitting cross-legged as the world rushes by,
I pull up in an instant,
But then they start to fly,

I grow those wings immediately,
Exhilarated in the aqueous sky,
I see them dropping gaily down,
As I continue soaring high.

My heart is turning into steely stone,
Heavy but ablaze with the burn inside,

It sets like the sun on the horizon of my
stomach,
Coiling with discomfort,
My mind cloying with shame.

Unwilling to look beyond the fence,
I have settled in all the humdrum,

Lost a little contact,
Just a little MINDNUMB...

What it is to me

In the twisted breeze of uncertainty,
There lies an inkling of hope
In the fuming rage of unbridled emotion
There lies a plea for help
In the acidic snaps strewn in playful humor
There lies a need to be heard
In the tease of jealous banter
There lies a request for reassurance
In the broils of heady passion
There lies an urgency of acceptance
In every small or meaningless scuffle
There lies a promise of reconciliation
In every moment of labored ignorance
There lies a demand for attention
In the interstices of revengeful silences
Their lies a compulsion to prove
In the bitter-sweet moments of love and hate

There lies a longing for permanence
In the warm contours of affection
There lies a shape of blinding trust
In the battle of trust and mistrust
There lies a chasm of un-resolve
In every prick of aching desire
There lies undaunted provocation

In each flash of fiery arousal
There lies a brave desire to deviate
In tiny moments of blushing innocence
There lays a child untainted
In every break-down of surrender
I wish you be my anchor
Every step I take away from this
I lose a little of my first love
I vent, I shout and I can't help but cry
Letting this go I don't even want to try
But things are bleak, all blurred ahead
All I have are tears to shed
But what I also have is that inkling of hope
That narrow flood of light, enough for me to cope
Because in every stretch of morose darkness
There lies the strength to escape
This can lead one anywhere
But it always leaves one in better shape
You are to me a world of dreams
I wish there was no rationality
That songs would play, that I drift in the air
And stay with you in entirety.

Interstices

A little something you read long ago,
Can be on your mind for years in a row.
It could be radical, it could be immaterial,
It could be rather thought-provoking or simply
philosophical.

One such thing was the concept of Interstices,
Tiny windows between two productive spaces.

Why it stuck, because it was a thing too close,
Too empathetic, too familiar, a little too close.

From this point on I would want it to be very
lyrical,
To explain this feeling & make it more relatable.

Going way back to our childhood, remember
that sweet phase?
When the lights went out & broke the daily
pace?

The homework, the housework, the mundane
chores,
All took a backseat without any fault of yours.
It was the force of the situation,
Not to be blamed on your lack of dedication,

It was a sweet spot in between,
Man-made failure & man-made routine.

Or remember the times when you are on the
way,
A long sweet journey on a blue, blue Monday,
Where you sit & wait for your destination
No qualms, no guilt about the lack of any action.

How about that time between two tasks,
Where you have no option but to wait for the
next ask,

Or the instance when you reach before time,
And have a peaceful waiting space before the
grind.

Or the stolen moments of seductive morning
slumber,
When the facilities are occupied & you wait for
your number.

A tiny window of rest in an elevator,
The lazy space through snoozing an alarm from
now to later,

The initial days of a long deadline,
The waiting in a never-ending long line,

Ranging from days to microseconds,
These Interstices are little presents,

In a chaotic, hectic world which refuses to stop,
So in this situation, don't let your spirits drop.

Think of this as a longer interstice,
Something we crave for, something we will
miss,
In small & big moments find your peace,
Find your little window, that moment of release,
From all the negatives that cloud the world,
From all the fear & panic that has unfurled.
Nature needed a break & maybe mankind too,
To heal a planet that's been more than slightly
askew.

Uncomplicate

It often feels like life is no longer linear,
It's branching out…
Into irrelevant corners, into a frenzied bout,
The mind feels unsettled, like a restless limb,
Moving without purpose, but moving on whim,
The desire to do something meaningful,
The miscarriage of each attempt to understand
'meaning',
The sheer dependence to feel gratified,
The need for attention, direct or implied,
The strong cognizance of what is harming you,
The stronger rebellion to still continue,
The intensity towards the idea of love,
Yet the insincere effort to justify that love,
The beguiled attraction to complications,
The holding on to precedents & obsessions,

In a world where being simple is frowned upon,
Where unassuming is a lack of opinion,
Where nice is interpreted as naive,
Where satisfaction is construed as no ambition,
Where settling down is a lack of drive,
Where false pretenses gather success,
Where honesty is a bad idea & humility even
less,
The world may progress, but the mental turmoil
will get worse,
Looking ahead? No, I want things to reverse,
I want to go back to a simpler time,
I want to be happy without any reason or rhyme.

Sullied Reality

It's this thing that I do and I do it too often,
I live to look forward or just reminisce the
forgotten,

The forgotten, the foregone, the discontinued
actuality,
So much so that, what's here & now becomes
'Sullied Reality'.

The mind wanders like a parched, erratic nomad,
Frenzied & tense, scurrying yet intense,

Settling sporadically in places of darkness,
In hopeful doorways of the future or in the
palpable cocoon of nostalgia.

The concept of *now* shortens with every little
venture,
It turns into *what next?* or into *this is such a
short-lived adventure*.

The penchant for something new far outweighs,
The happiness of getting something you have
been pining after for days.

The avarice for more, tenaciously defeats,
The blessed contentment of living a life of ease,

The unstoppable urge to measure success,
Makes one blind to their little triumphs &
progress.

If only *living in the moment* was more than just a
fancy notion.
If only one could catch each fleeting moment
with the same sincere emotion.

Would it not be wonderful to be able to uphold
the gift of existence,
The gift of experience, the interplay of ups &
downs, the beautiful balance,

So if one could think of life as an elaborate,
perplexing Jigsaw,
And all the moments one gets as tiny puzzle
pieces,

One needs to match those tabs to those blanks &
make sense of it somehow,
And the time & place to fix this tainted reality is
nowhere but here & NOW!

Between a Rock & a Hard Place

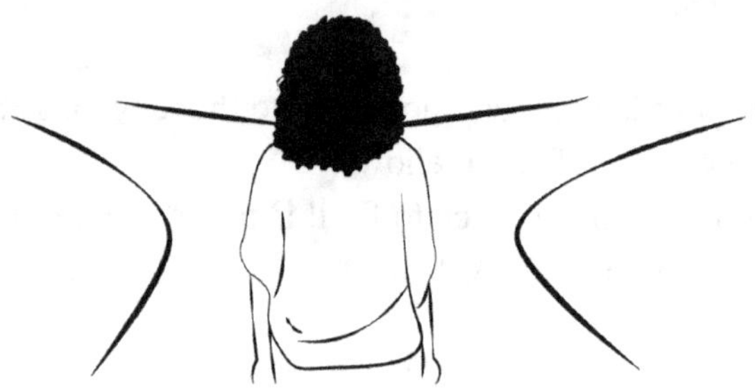

If hope is a crutch,
hindsight can be a bitter strain;
If knowledge is a blessing,
too much information is a bane;

If happiness is a state of mind,
dejection is lurking intently behind;

If getting something right is a thing,
why is regret constantly lingering?

If positively is the correct point of view,
why does superstition drive it askew?
If the state of rest is peace,
why does it bring overthinking & unease?

If looking forward to something is invigorating,
why is the real thing mostly underwhelming?

If being understood is what matters,
why is being desirable so sought after?

If achieving goals is a measure of success,
why is happiness such a prominent index?

If suffering is the ultimate low point of
humanity,
why is empathy in scarcity?

If loving someone is the foremost compliment,
why is it embroiled in passive-aggressive
detriment?

If simpler things give more comfort,
why are complexities only increasing in the
world?

If fantasies provide a vicarious escape,
why is realism the trending trade?

If individuality & choices are really important,
why is the encroachment so blatant?

If everyone has a different journey,
why the expectation for conformity?

If we look very closely, we will find,
each one of us is undergoing a different grind;

Some have it easier, some get a harsher share,
some deal with it better, some give in to the
scare;

Some can move resiliently forward,
some back step from anything untoward;

Yes, in an ideal world, everyone would be brave,
everyone would be in charge, yet they would be
tame;

But what we live is a subjective life,
with different struggles, different strifes;

Each point of view ready to justify their own,
each ambitious drive ready to fight for the
throne;

Each righteous self ready to preach,
each treacherous soul ready to breach;

Each benevolent creature ready to extend aid,
each miserly rogue active & unswayed;

Your best bet is to find your space,
between a rock and a hard place;

A fair and neutral ground,
which you religiously follow until the world
comes around.

Restless

Do you sometimes lay awake at night,
and feel slightly hollow, a little empty inside?

You wonder if you have any thoughts or ideas,
Beyond those augmented by the internet or
social media.

You wonder if you have learnt anything new,
amidst the mindless scrolling views.

You wonder if you are still capable of patient
introspection,
beyond the feverish, content-induced addiction.

You wonder if your day-to-day actions,
represent you or your thirst for traction.

Don't you feel you were once a deeper soul?
capable of feeling things in their true, authentic
whole?

Do you sometimes realize that all your thoughts
are half-hearted,
attempting to bloom but quickly thwarted,

in this vast sea of hollow distraction
which pulls you in despite all the passion.

Are we truly living like we imagined once upon
a time?
when we were young & honest & truly sublime.

But the paradox remains within us always—
do we restrain or let the world change our ways?

Because when you move forward,
it's a half-dystopian world with multiple
pleasures to explore,

But when you move back,
it's a long-gone memory whose return you can
only implore!

Tales of Time

The relativity of time is truly hard to deny,
Sometimes even a moment passes unhurriedly,
While a year vanishes in the blink of an eye,
A uniform piece of cloth in the fabric of time,
Bundling into itself
Moments & dreams,
Hopes & grand schemes,
All those oversights waiting to be redeemed,
All the joys & laughter & milestones vying to be
achieved,
All those improvements & changes to be
perceived,
All the perilous negativity eager to be freed,
The prospect of sweet fruits from sowing that
new seed,
That feeling of new, leaving the old to recede,
It's like crossing a fence unto that greener side,
Like fighting a wave & beating a tide,

Of life, of time,
Fooling yourself to believe in a new paradigm.

But as they say that your life is a creation of
your own mind,

A mind that believes,
Attracts a life that receives

Is manifestation real?
Do we truly have that superpower?

We are but blips in a vast universe,
A thought we think can spring to life,
An ardent wish may never see the daylight,
Our mind's telescope can sometimes experience
the fantastical phenomenon of 'Deja Vu',
While sometimes our memory fogs up on
something read moments ago,
Sometimes we concoct the most intrusive
thoughts in our heads,
Yet the same head goes blank when into a
moment of import it treads,

Sometimes a moment seems longer than an
eternity

Sometimes a moment is just that—a moment

Sometimes a large chunk of time shrinks into
triviality,

Sometimes that long period gives us a chance to
comprehend, to amend & alter our reality.

Is time a player or are we playing with time,
With our intricate little minds?

It's curious, it's baffling, it's really something to
ponder,
They say time will tell,
But it is our mind's extent, which is not a thing
to squander...

Little Things

Why did we stop talking about the little things?
The little things that build a day
The slice of sunlight bathing your room,
The happy song in your head you hum in tune
An old book that you can re-read,
A window in the day to snuggle into bed &
gobble a little treat
That momentary victory of completing a task,
That momentary breather during the day that
you wish could last
Words of simple praise can make or break your
day,
A good talk with your loved ones can obliterate
all dismay

A toothy smile from a little one,
An expected hug from someone you love
Buying a little trinket that makes you smile,
Watching a little something that transports you
for a while
A surprise sunset with orange & purple skies,
The sweet sounds of chirpings & bird cries
A silver lining illuminating a little cotton cloud,
A full moon resting in the night sky, so perfect
& proud
A bite of your comfort food,
A tune that matches your mood,
A good conversation,
A pretty illustration,
Some idle doodling,
A lot of canoodling,
All little, simple & small,
But when part of a day, they elevate all

Look from afar & you might miss them,
But it's the little things that really matter when
you close in the distance.

Perils of a New Mother

When did this happen, when did things change?
When did being the perfect mother become all
the rage?
From family to friends to strangers on cue,
All eager to claim that they know better than
you,
And yes, you are new to this, you need all the
aid,
But help should come with humility, not like a
painful grenade,
She has reaped her child with as much love &
care,
As any onlooker with uninvited words to spare,
She is lost at sea, amid waves of new
experiences,
Difficult to navigate, almost impossible to steer.

She is doing her best, devoid of rest,
She is bearing her soul, to fit that new role,

She challenges her limits, tries to strengthen her
spirits
She nurtures her child, while crying on the
inside,
She has support, yet she is alone on that boat,
That boat that's treading on turbulent waters,
Weathering the worst, yet journeying to the
clears
Journeying towards motherhood, the greatest
destination of all,
But to get there it takes time & tricks &
overcoming of all the pits & falls

As giving birth is not the same as becoming a
mother,
It's the acceptance of a new way of life,
New use of time,
New role to fit,
New mountain to summit,
She is hurled into this & yet expected to smile,
To be happy & thankful & rise above this trial
If only there was some empathy, some true
understanding of her state,
Some real conversations, some counseling, some
genuine will to educate
Some unconditional help, not vile or seeking
appreciation,
Some leeway, some room to be able to become
that person.

Less judgement, more awe
Before she can withdraw
Into the lonely world of mothering a child
Let her go, be free to explore, like a lioness in
the wild.

Through the eyes of a Non-Extremist

I feel strongly...

About equal rights

About men & women having equal lives

About sharing responsibilities, sharing strifes

About breaking the dogma that cuts so deep

About the obscurantism that runs beneath

About the lack of respect for a woman's body & life

About the little things & big things & the
multiple issues that thrive

But just strong feelings don't help anyone in any
way

I look, I feel, just a spectator at bay

I might sympathize, empathize, maybe shed a
tear alone

But it's momentary, a flash & then I just revert
back to my comfort zone

I feel strongly...
Or maybe I just think I do...

Treasures of Travel

Travel plans are more than a vacation,
They are an entity on their own,
Living & breathing, enticing your thoughts,
Hobbling into your mind at the most salient
times,
They give you a break before they even begin,
The planning & discussions transport you from
the daily din,
The prospect of change, a detour from the plain,
An escape from reality, a break to realign sanity
Not only that but so many ancillaries,
The propaganda & the validations,
The topic coming up in ever other conversation,
The drifting of the mind into an alternate plane,
Picture perfect in your head, by mere shift in
terrain
The excited frenzy of packing your bags,
The nervous energy of flying off somewhere
new,
The bustling curiosity to discover wonders anew,

There is self-reflection that comes in the laps of
nature,
A calmness, a serenity, a silent blanket of
emotion,
Or sometimes there is extreme romanticism,
In places with a pulse, with culture & wisdom,
Sometimes there are stories, hidden in the
crevices of that place,
Sometimes the stories are displayed to devour
inside a museum or a palace,
Oh, the adrenaline rush to catch that train,
To walk here, to tread there, to peak into every
wayward lane,
Oh, the joy of capturing moments as
photographs,
To fit yourself & the sight you behold,
To be able to carry it back in its essence, show it
to everyone, young & old,
Because a part of travel is the experience for
your soul,
It seeps into your being, it becomes part of your
whole,
But some parts are for sharing, the visuals & the
stories,
You want it to translate to anyone who is
collaborating with your memories,
The treasures of travel know no bound,
It makes you believe that home is not just on one
ground.

Fidget

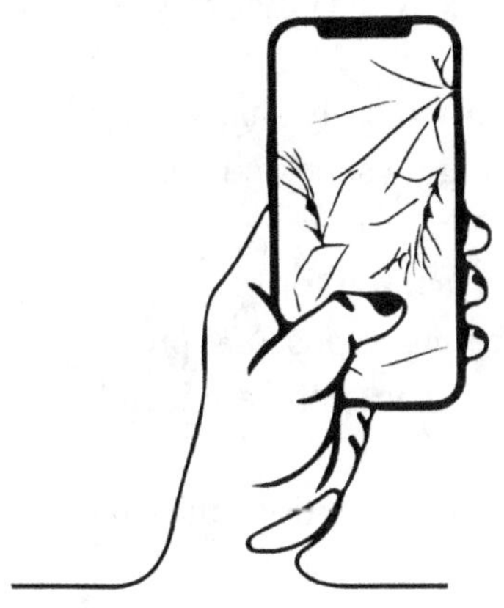

Can I sit still? I think not
Because I feel everything, at once & a lot,

When I sit with some work, my lips feel dry
I run my tongue across it, but then my hair feels
awry,

I tie it up to expose my neck, & I start feeling a
draft,
I loosen my hair, & just then I remember
something from the past,

I dwell on it, for a little bit,
But then I try to move on,
Just then my fingers twitch, my eyes itch &
I can't seem to leave it alone,

If I am not cracking my knuckles,
I am fidgeting with some knobs & buckles,

If I am not mindlessly shaking my legs,
I am doodling on speckled coffee dregs,

If I am not reaching for my phone,
I am just feeling exposed & prone,
To living the moments I am ideally supposed to
live,
But these tiny distractions provide that little
shift,
It feels like the body is begging you to move,
To break this monotony, to break out of this
banal groove,
I move & I twitch, but I try not to quit,
My fidgety mind might not settle all the time,
But a little pebble to ruffle still water, is just a
sign of life...

A Woman

A woman on her own,
Is not a woman who is alone,
She is a force of nature,
Strength bellows inside her,
There is not a thing she cannot do,
No adversity she cannot subdue,
She can reason, she can counsel,
She can sustain against her will,
She can nurture, she can birth,
She can give, without awareness of her worth,
She can love so much, it's hard to match,
She can build a home from scratch,
She can be powerful, She can be meek,
She can soar atop the toughest peak,
She can create ripples as she strides,

Or she can be the calmest creature wading
through the tides,
She can channel her best,
Or she can put her potential to rest,
Depending on who needs to shine,
That's how she & her family intertwine,
But why was an entity with such extremities,
With so much power & so much grit,
So much versatility, so many gifts,
Made physically & emotionally weaker?
Why did nature construct her so?
Why is she, the creator herself,
Overpowered by a man, his strength & his self,
Why make a feminine energy, if it was not
meant to be protected,
Why make a male entity if cannot be limited?
The difference in nature, is truly a thing of
wonder,
It should create that perfect balance,
But just like a woman is bound in her ambit,
Wish there was also a confine for men & their
gambit.

Unwavered

Untethered, unwavered, undeniably unscathed,
I wish I could be someone so strong, someone so
unapologetically unabated

Rising to the occasion in the face of adversity,
Quick on my feet to absolve any perversity

Oblivious to my weaknesses, always playing to
my strengths,
Obilerating obstacles, going to extreme lengths

Live life on my terms, with not a care in the
world,
Astute & brisk, ready to take a risk,
Move away from the race of the ordinary,
The race of likeability, to do what's necessary

Wish I could face the prospect of flying high,
Not be someone that any stranger can edify

Not mince words, just think straight,
Be polite, be kind but never politically correct

Be bold, be wild, to not be beguiled,
By the comforting charm of pleasing a crowd

Rise above this clout, be able to stand out

Untethered, unwavered, undeniably unscathed in
the throes of adversity,
Unbothered, unshaken, not ready to be broken &
be unabashedly ME...

Sublime

Imagine waking up to this pleasant rainy day,
The light whisper of drizzle & delicate spray,

You tilt your head backwards & bend into the
outdoor,
You feel the cool breeze caress your face, slide
into every inch & pore,

Tiny droplets of water pattering on the edges
Misty shrouds of rainwater bathing the corners
of your ledges,

That overwhelming joy starts at your wiggly
toes, & spreads through your whole body,
Your eyes close up, & gently so, as that feeling
you accept & embody,

It's nature's gift amidst mediocre times,
To give you a day so sublime,
When it's neither too harsh, nor too extreme,
When all forces of nature perfectly team,
To create this harmony so pleasantly surprising,
When Mother Nature & Man are simultaneously
thriving,

Just then you leave the outdoors to heal &
breathe,
Withdraw into your cozy home, your warm little
sheathe,

You take a deep breath & thank the stars,
Because a day like this can heal emotional scars,

You light up that stove & leave some milk to
bubble,
Add your sweet-scented coffee as the milk
doubles,
Add those clear crystals of caramely sugar,
Pour into a full-bodied mug with excited fervor,
Sit down with it with a lot of calm,
Treat your eyes to the outside, no regret, no
qualm,
And wish for another day amidst these mediocre
times,
For Mother Nature to give you another day so
sublime...

Dancing Feet

Dance a little before you head out, they say,
It makes you seem a different way,
When you move without restrain,
An unearthly energy slides into your veins,

It gives you a groove,
a style, a verve,

A cloud under your feet,
a little tune, a little beat,

When the music wades into your ears,
It stirs up waves, kickstarts your gears,

It washes the drab with a splash of fun,
It makes you want to be nice to everyone,

When you walk along with a tune in your head,
You feel like the main character, just strolling
ahead,
Towards a brighter, chirpier day,
Where there is no room for gloom, but joy can
overstay,

With dance you can succumb to sweet melodies,
It's exhilarating, it's satisfying, bringing you
giddy peace,

Dance, they say, is like dreaming on your feet,
Creating all the magic, before your mind
retreats,
Prance & sway, just dance away,
To beauty, to love or even just a slightly better
day...

YOU

When there is a crinkle on my forehead,
Those lines of worry or disdain,
I look for YOU to ease my pain

When there is a blip between a smooth ride,
That patch, untamable & grey,
I seek YOU, to get me through,
To the better side of the way

When there is defeat in my steps,
That dragging hope & feelings of regret,
I turn to YOU, to help me start things anew,
To help me unfog, to help me forget

When there is a time, I step out of line,
I make mistakes that cannot be undone,
I trust YOU to show me the right path,
To let go of the grudges, let go of the wrath

When there is a time self-worth leaves my side,
I feel stripped of all hope & pride,
I look towards YOU to gain back some
perspective,
To bring me back that hope, real or subjective
When I feel life is not treating me right,
It's giving me anxiety, it's giving me blight,
I move across to YOU for that light,
My pillar, my strength, to lift me back upright

When I sense sometimes that there is distance
from you,
When things between us are tinged with blue,
I still only have YOU to give me that reason,
To make things better before the gash deepens

So when I see myself, I also see YOU,
YOU who always comes through,
As part of me, as part of my whole,
A comrade, a companion, just everything to my
soul

Standing outside a Story Book

I turn the pages of a beautifully bound book,
Worn out & withering from the experiences of
being read,
Turned over & over by frantically excited hands,
By a fantasy-starved soul, eager to understand,
Are fairy tales only exist in stories, or do they
live outside?
Those castles, those bridges, those princes
astride?
But the dream is not just to be a damsel in
distress,
Waiting to be rescued, some helpless princess,
As I stand outside this wondrous storybook,
Pulsing in magic, drenched in imagination,
The illusion is to step right inside those pages,
Become a resident of that world, those unseemly
ages,

Eye everything, all the little details,
The beauty of words transformed into tales,
Soak in the vision of the author's mind,
Enter their world, the realm they designed,
To walk across the beaten road,
To a make-believe world
Touch those crevices that make these walls come
alive,
Take in the scent of those fragrant wisteria
miles,
Sit by a brook, breathe the freshest air,
Untainted by the outside, as pure as nowhere,
Maybe let a bird glide down to my arms,
Or even follow honeybees happily buzzing in
swarms,
Or just trinkle into my dwellings so warm,
Try on that shoe that can only exist out of
norms,
Or put on a dress so prettily tailored,
By some dressmaker while he was humming a
delightful ballad,
Or maybe I could check all the nooks &
crannies,
What trinkets, what baubles, what quirky kids or
grannies,
Has the author invited to his world of fancy,
Touch them, greet them, just experience their
journey,

I, the one standing outside a storybook,
Waiting to be engulfed into that otherworldly
nook,
I have set it aside, but the fantasy has not died—
Maybe the next one will take me in its stride.